Free Verse Editions
Edited by Jon Thompson

LAST MORNING

Simon Smith

Parlor Press
Anderson, South Carolina
www.parlorpress.com

Parlor Press LLC, Anderson, South Carolina, 29621

© 2022 by Parlor Press
All rights reserved.
Printed in the United States of America
S A N: 2 5 4 - 8 8 7 9

Library of Congress Cataloging-in-Publication Data

Names: Smith, Simon, 1961- author.
Title: Last morning / Simon Smith.
Description: Anderson, South Carolina : Parlor Press, [2022] | Series: Free verse editions | Summary: "Last Morning marks a shift away from poetry of place to the poetry of space: how poetry creates its own space, through its unfolding through time and space, and what kind of a politics, and what kind of a gift that might be"-- Provided by publisher.
Identifiers: LCCN 2021044305 (print) | LCCN 2021044306 (ebook) | ISBN 9781643172828 (paperback) | ISBN 9781643172835 (adobe pdf) | ISBN 9781643172842 (epub)
Subjects: LCGFT: Poetry.
Classification: LCC PR6069.M5465 L37 2022 (print) | LCC PR6069.M5465 (ebook) | DDC 821/.914--dc23
LC record available at https://lccn.loc.gov/2021044305
LC ebook record available at https://lccn.loc.gov/2021044306

978-1-64317-282-8 (paperback)
978-1-64317-283-5 (pdf)
978-1-64317-284-2 (ePub)

1 2 3 4 5

Cover photograph: Felicity Allen
Cover design by David Blakesley.

Parlor Press, LLC is an independent publisher of scholarly and trade titles in print and multimedia formats. This book is available in paperback and ebook formats from Parlor Press on the World Wide Web at http://www.parlorpress.com or through online and brick-and-mortar bookstores. For submission information or to find out about Parlor Press publications, write to Parlor Press, 3015 Brackenberry Drive, Anderson, South Carolina, 29621, or email editor@parlorpress.com.

Contents

Last Morning 3
   Post-Political Love Poem 5
   Elegy: On the End of Ending 8
   Fairground 10
   Aura 13
   Winter Poem 15
   Source Material 16
   Emergency Attention 18
   Afterlife 20
   To the Flag 21
   Song with No Reply 23
   Lyric 25
   Last Morning: Pastoral 27
   Almost Spring 30
   Essay: On the Edge of Ending 32
   (New Year) After Rain 35
   Cadenza 36
   Later Than After 38

Poetry's Space 41
   Lyric, an Explanatory Note 43
   Conditional 46
   Twenty-Seven 49
   White Giraffe 51
   Cell 54
   Loving Poem 56
   Great North Road 58
   Terms and Conditions 63
   Fact: Rain 65
   Angel 67
   History of the Pocket 70
   Sixty-Six Valentines 73
   Poem Without Pronouns 77
   Leading Edge 80

Second Song Book: Series of Songs 85
   Song: Call Centre 87

Song: Lyrik *88*
Song: Edge *90*
Song: Response Unit *91*
Song: Tear *92*
Charm *94*
Song Song Song *95*
Song: Return *98*
Song: Likeness *100*
Personal Song *102*
Shout: A Song *104*
Song: Mimesis *105*

Postscript *107*
   opens a space that touches *109*

Drafts & Fragments *117*
   Song: Cuttings *119*
   Passages Passengers *120*
   Song: Triangle *123*
   Reverie *124*
   Vital Signs *126*
   Envelope *128*
   Private Poem *129*
   Song *130*
   All Schubert *131*
   After After-Effects *132*
   Personal Poem *133*
   Sonnet *134*
   Song: Pattern/No Reply/Detour/Untrodden Path/Further Afield *138*
   From the Heart *139*
   Zone *140*
   On the Edges of Air *141*
   Alive *143*
   Lyric Bird *144*
   Pocket: Song *145*

Acknowledgments *147*
About the Author *149*
Free Verse Editions *151*

'you calmly open the door . . . . /the stars of lead/the stars of death'
— Jean Arp, from *Towards Infinite White* (1960)

'the sheer grace of wanting to give'
— Steven Madoff (2018)

Last Morning

Post-Political Love Poem

return of the World
footprints in the snow
across opened ground

stared out by the stars & the next question

year by year by year
yeah yeah yeah

the atrocities wear on
like weather
noise filled with noise

war in the sense
in the senses

& everywhere being broken
the correspondences the conversations
next question is next

raise the voice into space
all ozone
up up skylark

to the dark-edged heart

& the blue-black rain
& all the rest
blue-black

posthumous
witness
winter after

the word is late
the work is late

a broad day glows
with dead battles
& the wail of exiles

the something which truth once was
to the late World

the abode
witness

the looking hoping for a sign

under fire exhale & translate darkness

cloud thinning
noise filling air

threadbare as reportage
the holes the spaces

the poem Being
the field of living
turned open

images in hearing
its afterlife
an occasion as snow dissolves

this takes place in the senses
this takes the place of senses
& snow-blindness

posts or stations
some signs of activity radiant

articulations
in the sense in the senses
burns the mouth splitting at the seams

the republic awake to thunder
hazard & risk

& the living hand-in-hand with the dead
& the yet to live

this weather front this pathfinder
a step closer

the colour grey gives courage gives orange
& words bleed the look faded
the gone acoustic

the dream past stars
light left behind

Elegy: On the End of Ending

(for John James)

in gorgeous sky the church tower flowers with its corrugated roof
happiness like a charm of goldfinches pecking at warm tarmac

& no worries no blue where the air tastes clean
an open draft
they flit between

tangle
of long grass & brambles
in the uplift

the news like reading Hölderlin in the rain
turn into the bleak freezing air
or a silent walk mute & glazed

a long period of days
imminent immanence

keeping up keeping close to sunrise
rising on a cusp & never dies

attending as every bystander or interested party
on the tip of understanding

some sense makes no sense of the senses

when the words are holes
hesitant in the trick of it

the buzz in the ears endless reminder of the Infinite
in line & tone

a transport in the air unmoving
& way forward
full circle

autumn winter spring summer
o a beautiful country
full of the ugly

full of circuses & the right
breed of sentimentality
illusion full

to disappear to
a receding view

around the edges words shut off
fragment & fragment

for a tattered flag bleached white
& a swan's song

the lesson & the kiss after the next breath dwell
shown in building work lintel
doorway & leap

whisked by train to town
on the track of naming
the ground

digging back & back
further back
& further around

in the duration of the day shadow of the stars

'& your book resonant of a life'
enters the bloodstream clears the head & throat

deferred undecided
the closed not ended

Fairground

above tilted wave
one blue against ozone

the men on stilts
beyond the caravan park

sand & stars structure a totality of moments
above the tent
& mesh

or message in the inference
or off the deep & await the gods' return

among scots pine clearing
the edge of dream &
space

brick wall
all this mystery
& rough ground

circuses & tilt of wave
in a row

harlequin in black & white
tumble through air

seagull passing in forgetting
days turn

to data & the wind
the viewfinder finds insignificance
through gravel grass clumps

water's reflection up the seawall like flame

like rose
float up into "so there you are"
& "so who are you?"

to the north star
the net of the lyric in a pin of light

magicians shatter meaning into meanings

or how to read a forest
or a first view

like end of care tuned to a pneumatic drill
& the interference of the world
the open-ended left

over the immanent coming over
into clarity
refraction of view

saltimbanques charming the animals to life
agile awake all daylight

correspond to seeping half lit
into the path of shadows
& all the names missing

is to say something beside unfamiliar
& risk catastrophe

immanent in the process of constellation

sound
disappears as a pin of light
a hooded unknown

dreams disintegrating
echo receded
money in the meter

half-lit following pattern
between cracks
in shadow

stars embedded in air

what Orpheus didn't tell
the birds taught the poets to sing
correspondence

is a mere sign
saying goodbye

left as relics
between a galaxy or cell

at the tip of the horizon
the ocean at the end of the road

Aura

if what if
were the rule
& calm the same

& to learn each particle
connected to each part

if the poem were a measure of belief
or disbelief
or love

what then for Truth
or against
a ladder

or like a broken door leant against
building & forming letters

down the side of an arcade
what seems & is the impossible
pushed away

what defying gravity can
or cannot save lives

language is memory
mistreats beauty

turning translation
into a prepared statement

piling draft against
a draft already adrift
of history

when all the great abstractions crashing down obliterate the particular
when the meticulous detail of living record is no good & won't save lives
when rock dust blasted through bodies forming barriers what then

a tidying of the end
of days ever alert
an angel passes through

non-terrestrial without rest without trial
without

everything in this vanishing act
the fleece & crease of it

the deportations

light the Truth of it

held to priceless ransom
etched in the names on air

Winter Poem

where the wound is

for the food & cash
the hunger

a road a hill a valley
downwind to town

for clarity cleared the way
scattered

light as a cloud
the puff of a cloud

pole star in the freezing midnight sky
clear as that

significance reads as red

the work of the lyric
the heartbreak to music

city light shattered
buildings concrete walls
cars passing ambulances

like reading the future
returns full circle

Source Material

looking out of the window
at all that is out of the window

sun slanted
slatted
& 'yes' as warmed brick

or grey pigeons their petrol feathers
absorbing the warmth as sadness

& the loneliness
of wind on a lone rose out there
tiles chipped & worn

to capture a drop of rain
tense lenses
in the tyranny of the immediate

& from a small room
cooped in a small room

emerging from a broken ecstasy of sight

is to exist on the edge tipping forwards
on a wavelength or bow

web to a signal tracking like a drag anchor
an arc

invisible corona to the sun
& memory

the fiction of it close to the burst of time
busted down
precarious between

touching ground & air
electric with risk
into flare

as news is a hard run thing
ragged of fact & already
long gone

into other pasts
into other darknesses
& knocks at the door

is to look back into the interior
to the cells of the brain
synapses between

song aware
playing the cards
a call out to hollow data

where Reality is worn through
& an excuse to say it plain & true

pulled aside to the twinned twined

the gods never more contingent
in the flash & bang of risk

the dream of dreams & the waves of waves

Emergency Attention

is lyric flowered into realignment
without content
like a leaf's wing

the self edge

the record straight
a mouth touched by a moth
the full call

pull away the netting
pull away the haze

the stranger in your face
even through a veil

the Truth is blue broad
daylight azure through

ultramarine
through gauze

word without heart without

it cannot say it
with a wish lapse & cell

centrifuge & definition
recalls all forgotten thought
not quite quit

kite fanned tail feathers
silent dips & holds the air
above the glaze

reconnection of nowhere
above rooftops fields left
to fallow

to right its shadow free
form its eclipse
elapse erase

crystals of sand one answer
blown far

you see yourself
other bodied other

in a borrowed light the breach flowers
alien shadow stranger

collapsed no refuge now here
none no-one to wander in mind of

the envelope of light
the envelope of presence
to midnight right there

in earshot on twigs hedge sparrow
the veil quiet

to sing to live "live"
turns the coins to good

not simple work
life & death
turn breath

picture by picture by picture
window after window after window
time captured

the cold cold enough for snow
in its shadow wounds opened

wonder sung out
& wrung

believe the World the flowering mouth
an impossible levitation

Afterlife

as if in the corner of the room
the corner of the poem
the corner

the first letter first
contact
beneath that space

the tongue holds open

the space the spec
as if luminous
outside the window

opens the corner the glade open
into the firs into the pines
beside the track

lit
the black & green
as if poplars dotting

the air poor eyes
know things
don't

open

like lemon rape seed through fog
as if degrees of shadow at variance
pitch

attests
fields marked up as tattoo
as shadow

its open hum
tipped out of like
poetry's space 'as if'

To the Flag

is the ghost in the narrative

the Holy Grail is one of these
& grows like a virus

like echoes
for no turning back
& real as a cup of tap water

as real as naming a form
of recollection
with the accuracy of care & grace

& what is good for the heart

of human dust
the dawn blue still night
with no incidents to report

from the first the swallows flit & mew

force-field / constellation / star

from the first resist attention
flashback as headlights
the dark floating out there

haunted by the Real
suspended
all thinking done

as closing points
lean towards consequence
the bluer skies are now

& dreaming hard
of folded possibilities

things things things the wreckage
paying with the sentence
its currency

wrapped up in the flag
all the dead
in its recoil

& God is an it
as the present tense

adds up to simple dissent

field guide / drums / mouthings

& to forget
what to see exit

emptied as an envelope
of nothing left but to follow
hollowed away

of not quite yet
to hold back refuse the gap

or the route back
to the loved ones who only sit it out
in sorrow & loose ends

with the freedom to walk the streets
& the freedom to walk away
to wait up for the return

an exhalation an 'ah'

the ghost is a kind of cold angel
to see what is being done with
& fits like a bent key

when there's no more honey in the world

a full-moon tracking right
& what is good for the hurt

the personal song that breathes the flag of disobedience

lets all the air & light in

Song with No Reply

the mirror swallows this side of the World

assemble a smile assemble a simile
behind the rain

applied pronouns to make the picture is making Love
the stars in the night skies are actors

the earth in shadow
the angel returns
& shadow

the sorrow & alienation of white shapes

awaiting Heidegger's call
with keys & stars & birds
a piercing light

the birds this side little different
from the birds that side
ghosts down the tramlines

cut through the north turn
pitched
dropped in a pool to no reflections no adjustments

& away from the edges the unicorn
item item purple blossom
& the centaurs & mermaids return

a poem with all the pronouns switched off
the white stone below the oval window
the prose of the body keeps notes to self

the love in the music of the voice
when there's no hope except the last instance

another side of the mirror
secret secretion unpicked
its broken music

the murdered for doing nothing
wait yes wait
in overheard articulations

the earth in darkness
swallows broken music

Lyric

looking at "you" as a sign
& "liking"

is to think of the lyric & bird
as breath as self dissolves on winter air
on the "if" as in gift

echo not far off
holding breath

the air silver electric
elemental need
& how light is

is a wound held open by a word
in the green or was it
blue twilight

"I" this constant reinvention
take this opportunity to wave to "you"
hanging around corners & wide-open spaces

in the present tense
close as breath
& the sky moves unnoticed

as a wave breaks over
a wave

conditional in the countdown of minutes
moments seconds
"as if"

the place of the suspended
below bellowing
or the air swallowed

concealed in the ordinary day
& here is "I" bullet to the past
in the politics blooded the mouth

in the buff of manila envelopes
singing into a cry

a calling into the word
at the doorway

venture out & the moon shifts
so late the arrival
& the World

the dawn blue then always blue blue
blue black & creeping chill

the "like" left hanging
some escape to exile
& occupy the "if"

the cells replaced in the body every seven years
like light bulbs so who am "I"
close as breath & closing

off the grid & in the end

Last Morning: Pastoral

I. REPORT ON LIMESTONE

up the lane hearing voices
the clouds the blue of the sky the rainbow
emanates from a crag

swifts dart above firs & pines
the third short-wheelbase Land Rover over the cattle grid
bottle-green & down from the shoot

a chaffinch pecking among stone chips
outside the Spar
doomed to material need

branding brands the land
in the quiet dead partridge
scatter B roads

the smell of rotten eggs hangs
all the rats & foxes of the imagination
jackdaw rook or two

heading back down the tilt of the track
settlement below
light breeze & a slight chill

farmed trout for tourists
pheasants corralled for game
flushed squawk from the copse

sun horizontal to the horizon
the song alert & fresh
& the report of twelve bore across the valley

greetings from chickens & baby rabbits

three cars all day no walkers
rain the odd spot

limestone cottage backing onto limestone quarry

behind a dry-stone wall
sheltered in the suntrap
crouched out of the wind

with laptop & smartphone
snapping snaps

hens chirp along to say "hello" second day running

picking through lines
& jotted field notes

& concentrate half a cold cup of tea
for a passage from *Zhivago*

the weekend shoot off-road
& scented diesel
a painted lady common tortoiseshell

sheep coaxed from field to field
chased by collies up the ginnel
the sun dropped behind the fell

the rasp of the wheel
a potter throwing pots

II. ON THE HILL

return to
& a hike up the lane
turn

light off the tarn

glass of water beside me
unhurried hand
safe as a café

& the Spar
delivers its promise
the three fat hikers look on in disbelief

musicality in its ruin
the homing aim of rain

III. HAPPY

trying to be less unhappy I promise

like omens & sonnets
refusing to die quite yet

sunshine punishing
deep into tarmac
heat fills the lungs

this life like a tictac box
that life over
the horizon the tangible edge

hand-in-hand touching the gods

the Escort growling in reverse

& in time
to the acid erosion
of administration

Almost Spring

a tree growing out of a roof
& the days flicker away so fast
flushed clean with rain & finished

is to be municipally cleansed with the early morning glow
is to almost walk away unharmed but full of chill & abundance
& the scent of wisteria sweet & easy as that

& the well-married doves coo gliding down the wires of silence
the boulevards warming to affluent peace

& blossom the tone of flesh
a sample a specimen to fall outside the plain white frame of likenesses
a cloud suspended

half behind the roof half
not blindsided & beside the social contract

is to be nudged to be reminded
oh yes the unbearable loneliness
when the gods were lost *that* Truth

& the Love impossible where the leaf unfurls unfolding pasts
passed into memory
to too quickly follow entanglement

& the end of forgetting
like the covenant of trust broke long ago

warning & metaphor mattered
muttered as much

beyond the streets boulevards city limits
an island broken off a continent

a gull floats silent & above alone

& through the grey gloom out there
off a cliff
eye level level of the sea

as rain threatens
then comes down

first a diaphanous mist then hurried showers
droplets airborne enveloped in a kind of moan

the trajectory down by pull under

underground to the Underworld

when in the World & in the morning
terns regroup float the air silent as arrowheads
above then across marshes on the other side

the grass purpled again & again
sunlit horizontal & as far as the horizon
dark line through the picture

its material & trust what shines & what leaks back
what draws blank

what seemed in pattern
to hold promise even
meaning holds none to overflowing

within earshot launched toward the ear
spoken alive as an olive
out of memory

speaks into the silence & the stuff where it belongs
to know how sound sounds
with what's left lying in the lyric

Essay: On the Edge of Ending

calling back to song calling

at the end
this year's Perseids shower whoosh
invisible through daybreak's grey-clay sky

the hours folding over hours
& over as if chance were waiting
the answers by a thread

the questions by the throat
snagged on the gaze

awaiting synthesis
its catharsis
& signature

song reads roads as reeds
the exile beside a stranger

one as secret one as chance
look
& how it sounds

driven cross-wise
the length of a country

as chalk clay limestone
the ground changes its meaning

weather its shade or light

the specks of dust
haunting private space
& points of travel

this end to the very last of it
in the trail & tail
all &

hunting out & pointing back
pointing the Universe
into cross hairs

& bearings turn by turn
the compass whirls round & round & round

the earth's magnetic field toppled

as tides recede
in the end of it

echoes answers
upended

questions & falling lines
as if in light coded
& failing

as if the tattered leavings are clouds

& the drift across
as if ghosting over with invisible dust like documentation as if
deranged & hemorrhaged

sunlit off white
cliff
as if a face a beacon a haunting

haunting ebb of the lighthouse
its regular pulse

code for the echo how it surrounds
this form this

from the cliff face
provisional & floating off

like cosmic dust in air
attuned

closer to attention
& closer still
of water white noise & space

the tune is up
as if of & off

like waves like radio
code for a provisional miracle

to witness
a wave come crashing down
measures between

stars & specks

whiteness & whiteness
between

witness & witness

boulders of chalk
horizon to a raised edge

blue eyes like granite in the field
the assassin's time is up
click stopwatch to tip or turn

calm down come down & sit by the edge
& in the end this will have me burning up like thin air
& gone with song

out here margin or edge

(New Year) After Rain

the moon a sliver of silver
this early in the cycle thin
& the rush of tyres

when the message is the wind
the pivot & clatter
at the letterbox

formlessness coming over into form
made from the silences of clouds
crumpled papers a monogram

made of city light feuds
sparrow tweets
ambulance sirens

constellations both clouds & flowers

released into the next day
torn drawings & stars of light

already looking at a world

Cadenza

who will dice the dice
everything is this

the necessities of rain
trees about to talk

slip road tarmac steaming
grounded to forget the myth-making

discharged into the depths of things
forging a path through

the constant dive & climb
of swifts
shriek & final clarity

unstoppable in the air that connects
lifting the air

circulation through the one-way street

sound on sound
"you" are my lingua franca "you"
are

commute the feelings distribute the facts
copied & counted

of parked cars as lyric
remembers all the dead people
sing the broken

written with the heart or against it
what had meaning on the tip then lost it

the no one of the words
shadow or bodies flashing beacons
pinned in a question or muffled reverb

the shelter of the question
house & home
language is

a category of poetry
takes the measure
as a reading

as a seeing the wave as a hearing the wave

swift & nightingale out there
on the wing & exile

rock dust blown through bodies
as the dust on other planets is

a cave in the envelope of light
a door not shut still open

& how is light
how is music how is that
answer echo

with what floats out there & the consequences

of a wing its own fallen
pushed back the only space the voice
answer that answer

Later Than After

snow unsettles attention
now's straitening

& can a theory be a lyric
can a theory *Be*

like a shadow
like a dancer

one blown leaf the only sign

constellations turn
one edge of the field

the stratosphere
the state of exile

no dreams to nights no stars

frame after frame after frame
remainder is reminder

knock knock knock
turned

cold sinks & the easterlies
down from the lanes the paths

dry snow falling to dry
ground
fly & spread

& can a theory be a life-force
a turning out of breath
before last thoughts

the sons of stars
wind-whipped sown snow

in time there & back
straightening the path

no dreams no rights no stars
no way past no way

to find a way
life-force into leaves

Capitalism is loneliness
& all the meanings of "post"

& the once gone World
earth still there
turns the turn

upward up
the road skyward

breathe in artic air
on high attention on edge

Poetry's Space

Lyric, an Explanatory Note

stranger & wanderer riding the edge
for forgotten data with the signal gone

walking the rim at the end of the World walking

the centre the meridian the aura evaporated
halo cupped

the upturn to meander is
Being in the saying
in the end in the exile

language & tongue
the grooves followed round
capped

lyric put to death
cutting short a charm
as clip to clasp

pulling
broadcast into deeper night

above shout & echo
& echo of that shout
about cut calm

& out & drop away
put simply in small hours

turning out lyric thing
after liar for liar
caught in the music

full circle
before liar here then gone
silent to conceal its secret

circular
strange to the end of the delta

touched out of sleep
talisman or plumb line
gated cellular data

wind song strung out
tributary & estuary

& strong
snapped to attention

politics flagged for renewal & moving parts
layer on layer
shell brown field & lyre

song made up as it goes along

lyric living on is to call back
its own momentum

its own mountain
& conversation

cloud slight pink edge
edge to captured sunset
& to every outlet munitions or retail park

slightly out of shape
how to make the ordinary language
sing poetry's space

to its cell to its centre to its shimmer

lightning lighting conversely
shark tactic to secret burst
& lyric lie

faint glow close to source feint
tremor

living in the daylight & every second

where space is a cube not a square
strong in daylight
as "yes" a mark on paper

pulled taut & straight as a string of DNA

suspended in the living day
the meaning the heft slightly out of grasp

again to appear as shadow
not behind the eyes
beyond the tongue

Conditional

is to show in this space

as if conjured out of imaginings
hard as crystal

as energy itself as if
everything is this

hurled through the air like black sickles
the conditions of flight of if
of high & low

& if half-exposed as if
half-expressed

with language its dark window
sign & stone both

as if as though
to speak from the doorway

to swallow back down the air
in retrospect with reflection switched on
& earthshine away from the road

above airways above airwaves
radio traffic & noise
is neutral

the cut & risk
to choke the chorus & Orpheus

echo of Eurydice down below
& crumple the echo

the thing is the id or the res
in charge

the earth is not left
is not that which is
left Life guesswork is

explainable in the notes
& all the things unwritten
as if to

swoop round & shriek
dash into the ocean

when calm as a pillow of cloud

neat as a sachet
cruel with ambiguity & lyric
& what not to like

stones white with shadow
follow the signing path of the gods gone

so on the wave signaling
like a holding of the breath
in its edginess & distress

an envelope of sunlight
reflection reflecting
a filigree or corona to the edge

at the end
it's in the question not the assertion
like water

in the fabric & connection
with the sun's indelible yellow

see more see further to see
pushed away
half as if

to breathe out
is to sleep on the wing at ten & a half
thousand feet

as if to half inhabit the space
as impossible as communication is
+ or – positive or negative

gate & threshold between pillars
the 'as if' of quartz & granite

so who will dice the dice
solid as a shoe

Twenty-Seven

twinned voices sing
with it
where they're going

with the 'you' & the 'me'
split & twined

to return to the earth
to sit out the winter
along the permanent road

stop reflect move on
on thin air
quite startled into understanding

through the laptop
window on the world
this envelope of light

containing the unforgettable
& the forgettable

the gazed on in the gazed at
unfolded to form the 'we'

like a string twisted out the other side
like a poem
is a wardrobe & a wardrobe is a memory

& a memory a cloud
like a fingerprint

linked to a thread
each time twenty-seven comes around

caught in the moving colours & moving light
like the children here & the children gone

the asymmetry in family
that that language could be
Be Life with birds insects the animals & humans

living now & at the end of Time through fingertips
or twenty-seven
is as good as any number numbered & unoccupied

the very edge where the eyes grow accustomed
the window lit up & the rain all night

or the purity of impurity
away from the separated elements & chaos

what if what is taken away
is as much as what is given

& whatever couldn't be good couldn't be

soundings in both voices
this twenty-seventh day

White Giraffe

unknown
worked on in sleep

in new forms
the call of song

the ghosts rising & left

invisible to silence & silver
homeless in search of asylum
& trace

beginning to forget an afterlife beginning
in the idea of the edge
in the sound of falling

the unicorn's immediate first view
in the music in every muscle

a form of thinking
without Reality
ghostly luminous by night

& catastrophe
unfolds the necessary present
room by room house to house

with vibration & shimmer
echo sounding

words the measure & form of conveyance
into a synthetic discourse

birds & animals outside
the perfectly open sky
envelope ice-cloud & inlet

breath beneath them
a pocketbook of secrets

in the mirrors the waters the narrowing things

in mistakes
in misunderstandings
in misapprehensions

the unicorn
in the naming of things

in the calling the saying

the Sublime
goat or silver horse
or both

the intimacy & secret folding away
dream at ground level hidden from view
unfamiliar no return the gift

the perfectly open space
to think with

something that happens & shouldn't exist

as the present unfolds
then something does
white sounding

& speechless after exile
& the cold in the code
from altitude

reduced to chill
to dwell with the dawn
chorus

would be to stare into blue
displace floaters
white noise

to conceal the appearance
disclosing the concealed
merge with the page

cabbage whites are ghosts
& angels

like a glance in a glass
& the effect of affect
in call & dance

Cell

& all the wet trees

in this era coming to an end in this moment
the horizon of resonance
point of entry

stopping for lilacs & magnolia sunshine brings
more pollution smell of fumes

stood gazing willow out in the air

when a shadow appears as a fold
flexible as water

& in the corner of an eye
starting points are startling points

like the sound of a fountain clapping
as light sneaks under a door

there's your answer under erasure
& the air full of water

disappeared complete with the moment
& what narrative to attach
unresolved ground taking shape

around a hinge or tunings
no speaking language
of indeterminate area

be everywhere instantaneous

time magpies don't forget through enactment
delivering the letter
waiting the answer

new growth light defining
yellow flowering jasmine

a made-up thing
& cold of the ground

sells in this plastic flexible world
point of entry to the late word
broken song attending toxic

the broken sound in mud

as if by chance
exile at dusk

folds into distance
& infinite variation
the song

what runs through tuning tap by tap
each side

holds open the wound
second to second
is to close not to end

Loving Poem

filmic the liquid form of images forward
cutting through drizzly rain brightening air
in likeness in reproduction in closeness

in rain swept in on the tide
gulls & oystercatchers a curlew
the odd dead washed up jellyfish to add

through lens through window
the clear eye & clear idea

the stars start beyond
the one word left
out to the high winds

& a kind of love for the world

to die soundless on rushing air
wordless tongue in two

read through the edge of the edge of water
to go without

fallen open detoured
where things will move away
road railway line estuary

the photograph in accurate present
the acute present on breathable air
in loving

creation aura
change accompanied by shock
distraction besides concentration

other side to the railway embankment
the curlew defending territory & fishing
then a hill then a castle

in a hull in money worries set aside
in the great hall
the cacophony & serenade of curlews

light overcharged unaccountable
the nation like a creaking old boat
wind kicking at the end

its vanishing aura

just as the perception of the object
penetrates the thing

heartache & heartbreak it all ends in
the singing next door
forever ever sounding

down the branch line
& as everything between earth space
forms reality in this envelope rising & forward

where the fighter banks & flips the sonic boom
scatters waders & gulls

miracle bird thigh deep in local ooze
& first light

likeness reproduction closeness closed
light sleep terrible silence & buzz like the tides always there
checking back this is the dimension of water in the mechanical age

returned to particulars for which there are no uses
reproduction in replica design giddy with air
this is now this now is a 'love poem'

if only longing were where nothing much happens to nothing much
where stars are starts forever soundings brightened air

Great North Road

walked in uncertainty mystery doubt
each up
ended term

pilot as puppet as poet

suspended part
in part out part apart

momentary stopping point
white church tower
sun held to the phantom Spring

all day half done
conversation
taken

disappeared into darkness
night-air thin
breathed breath-fog

stepping outside
timed to the march

spread from the eastern boundary
the coastal turn
& marsh in between

the future where the birds not arrived
sing on a form of words opening light

even beginning a kind of ending
& no one listening
by the wayside

between heart & head heard deft

marched over the hill to the crown
over & out through airwaves

through endless snow
white on white on white

as ghostly to be that ghost
not I or you Being
falling silent or apart

stopping outside

for interval or breath
with an accent

in the covenant to dream
to meet up

along the top
road in shadow beneath the hill
shadow

singly singing
derived from drift
trooping north

as the crow swaggers
chatters its crow laughter

part corona all roads lead
in conversation shadow ahead
in terms turns away

ordered into another sea
& language
another shape

as words belong
elsewhere married to an idea
another space

leaving behind the left behind

in the grey language
the undefined language
of a china-clay sky

as words belong
false borders to cross
to the heart

network
arteries in the art
of circulation the coronary

by the second
the secondary beat
the second bypasses

beaten & how human voices are lost
to a show of hands

where conversation ends with transmission
& termination

the land & ground folds broken clocks
over a detour
itself dust

the data inscribed there

at the root of the road north
admits darkness only
rises as a cloud of gases rises

stopping stations
elliptic & a turn towards silence
of a crow hobbled flâneur

defined by line acid eating in
at the edges of daylight
song

is to repeat & cycle
circle

along the way to all conversation
sworn on the sewn mouth
by the words drift apart

friend or other in "mother"
disguised as corpses
winded floored

marched over the horizon to a crown
breathtaking day
recycled

floating to get here
where the future awaits arrival

where the message is
without flowers without song

in the cockpit of the helicopter
late turns later
posthumous

then over the hill & away

derived from drift
hours of daylight lost to winter

fall as these words
fall as these falsehoods
fall as physics fall out in phase in part

as paths
belong to someone else
in secret secretes language

accept & receive what is given
elsewhere
hidden in questioning

step into silence stop

read as road north
lost to the roar of aircraft

Terms and Conditions

inland one gull blown only one way to talk about politics
is the only way we are where we are
to lift free above phone wire

air & light
this is the snow falling downwind
one way only

like the gull on air
unpicks suspension

then tumbles away left
out of sight
fugitive

& in lines name a name or print one off
read them back the dead

featherweight along the border
of entanglements confusions suspicions

snowflakes stick to one place
& freezing rain snaps full-grown trees of limbs
crashed into echoes

& cold routine
trauma for the homeless the tidied away
politics through refrain

useless repetition lined up
committed to air & light
shock & manifesto

closed on silence clouds & touch
endless encounter around borders tied
to boredom

tired of the telling
to tell the truth as snowfall sets in again

stiffening wind
dimmed song muted cloud ice freezing rain

takes breath away
curling into blizzard whirl & drift

the snow fox come for food an explanation
sniffing the air for signs

a leaden cloud in the darkness
only a nomad can trust

tent on the edge of town
the tree a high hill & no language

Fact: Rain

selves hollowed out caves
into the curves of discourse
following the lines of light

on the looking out
answers await the collision
walking with an exile

the many voices of a city
clouds tilted above

drift
stand in the rain then walk away north

kept going
in the ascent the accent
& sing your heart out

to winds picked up then dropped
in the atom & storm

known in the months
from mouths by heart

whitenesses witness bird bones
wing in the distances without eye contact

hold the planet
to head to hand to heart

unsettles mud
weighted the full fall

at the fall emptying pitch
impossible to leave behind

song snagged on the throat
contingent interference
station turn breath

second to second
& understand the silence between
distance

wringing where rain rains is ruin
its under-breath edged
settles settlement

out wait the waiting
listen to the wind
the soft blue light

a form testifies to witness
displacement
a walk into exile

following lines of light
marked in the stones
in the clouds

stand by the rain the gap between

Angel

altitude is a form in the slope or tilt
in the shape
sown stars

the World that matters in the matter
o a little voice

speaker witness observer
the angel the bridge from here to becoming
to or cuts away cutting

to tow
from the centre
& the last to speak

about to disappear in a trick
of the light
& the experience of living through time

not the account of history
the anthem of forgetting

not a flag
drift & wandering but a note
the dance in correspondence

in this turning away of the World
this turning away of the gods
the knowing invisible

& not much sign of Spring
shattered & out of control

exterior altered
letter in the form of delivery
strange & stranger

big distance in the imagination
we are the same in the act of pure perception

as if the angel occupied the place 'as if'
tipping forward out of the corner of the eye
as a scene & a space unfold

material invisible
& minute repetitions along the journey

the abandoned wreck of the lyric

abandoned silences

& all the blossoms whirl
summer too soon
as if in the rush of what sounds like the wind

as if thinking clearly carefully around
thinking poetry's space
a poem would be an angel

in the shock of it
the dissent & distance

waiting to receive a call
the bitter angel the terrestrial angel

where all the energy runs
to greening fields to trees coming over into

to call out into that spot
the rising the rushing past
& out

aerial
a bird's penetrating cry a bird's
broken code

down the road the angel's muddy tattered wings
the dowdy reality
&

YELLOW

*the World in sodium light
hanging from streetlights*

*selling money
of little voice*

the remanent of song repeats through
in the drop
the epoch of memory becoming

the era of forgetting
following what follows

breath thin breath thinning

corralled & controlled to take leave
gradual departure

the same as the act
pure perception
& breathing

words leaving stranded the mouth of everyone

tumble through air
voice an angel's
haphazard without form

languages mouthings

open through a cloud
o voice correspondence

History of the Pocket

a shelter & a secret
a shifter

is to stand outside time
a ticket stub a laundry receipt
a micro-story

painted from memory
to seal & conceal
working on paper walking on

as a poem is a pocket & swifts' nest

a home a dwelling an echo chamber
an undisturbed crevice

& the cord is flying
as the scaffold breaks the sightline
under the house eave

air delicate habitat fragile

language a category of poetry fallen
from grace into a slouch
hands in pockets

sudden arrivals late April programmed for August departures
& two broods between
twin pockets

the DNA to overwrite its contents
eyes open mouth open
pillow of cloud

a cadence
as background information
all neat full & enclosed

carries through sound carries through
the back roads with blind sides

the weather & how to survive it
carries a packet lost in a pocket
of time

the swifts the screamers
precipitous migrant answerless
tipped around a day

this pocket or any
carries a packet
liminal

whose eyes form into a 'yes'
of luminous blue filaments
of common blue damselflies

triangulated between song & prose
cloud & sky

the encounter intact & last things
in hand
a pocketful of misunderstandings

wide as a picture window wide as a picture

framed a pocket branded 'pastoral'
unfurls to leaf cradle
sounding as though hidden

to leave as a secret
warm to warm the hands chilled
a slip of glove

how would a poem help
how much a pocket contain

a stanza is a room
tuned to a watering-can

Coda, or Pocket within a Pocket

you me & the language what are we going to make of it
poetry speaks to the truth of things as the pocket protects those things

poetry is the World as it tips over into the Real
or disappears into shadows or a pocket or the shadows of pockets
living through the age of what is pocketable lining the truth

Sixty-Six Valentines

1. a day of all days for Love poetry

2. snow & the very air too cold

3. to capture as a snowflake as a snow drop

4. peeks through the dark earth

5. & snow

6. because its no-one's birthday but Love's

7. & to love the invisibility of Age

8. to become fainter & fainter more

9. abstract to be aware of Abstractions

10. so here drifts a citizen here a ghost

11. there the lover there the adulterer

12. host to the what-was-then-&-the-what-is-now new

13. & sixty-six snapshots to the here & now

14. sixty-six snapshots taken to kiss your forehead

15. & any excuse

16. to list our loves all infinity of them

17. a place where words talk to one

18. & another lover

19. where Love is lost to Time

20. & another time

21. suspended in the air

22. where the song ends

23. & where the song begins

24. crazy like my blood pressure

25. with fizz & celebration

26. waiting for my head to stop

27. when all is forgotten with the end of Time

28. writing the seconds away

29. making sense of dreams

30. email conversation & formal letter

31. halfway between

32. when the frost on the glass

33. drawn in on the cold

34. drawn like a drawing is drawn

35. lyric without boundaries or reaction time

36. returning you back

37. to the word pops up as 'joyous' pops up as you

38. were a dream in a room & where the words are gone

39. where the dice were thrown

40. where as blackthorn winter blossoms in white

41. great clouds of the stuff

42. float upward as though through a dream

43. like memories like landscapes in memories

44. in touching distance

45. of Stanley Spencer's imagination where the creases

46. in your eyes were in a bracelet set with two semi-precious stones

47. in the form of balance before floating

48. balanced in the form of floating

49. Love where no lies follow

50. the cold cold & snow will snow snow

51. the flip to 'Winterreise'

52. or it could be an ode to joy

53. crazy as my heartbeat & irregular as yours

54. and the what-is-not-now

55. nor new nor the answer

56. when each destination is comes to be known

57. when dice are thrown

58. as we'll drink to that

59. as Catullus coins 'basium'

60. hidden or lost to the abacus

61. & not a hair on head or Berenice

62. a curl away to the constellation

63. & firmament Love unaccountable

64. or me sitting in this Paris hotel room

65. writing this to you so you'll know

66. Love where no lies can follow

Poem Without Pronouns

dice the dice
where solitude tips into loneliness
sea light & further afield

broken from the roots & foundations

discharged through heart & earth
to land overheard

in the distant whine of speedboats

turning descent to dissent
pushed back into the shape of the voice
maybe some small thing maybe

filled with relationship
in the bend of the arm

in the mis-heard in the miss
the narrownesses the straits

is to
talk through the poem without knowing it
bracket & caveat

cave in
the envelope of constant daylight edge
cutting forward

is to stand outside outside

of a ballooning sail
outside oh a zero a 0
shadowed fade on

a distant whine then a sign
a game of chance & a zone of waves
allowed to fail outside time

as multiple dials spiral
deal out multiple readings

out at sea out of air
& out of control conjure

what will exactly take precedence
dissolves in the face of the sun
into opening air

the long days lifting into

turning the present
in the pressurised cabin & cockpit displays
& to see where this is leading & landing

beyond the iced-up porthole
report what back into reality
the whole world rushes on

the fluid key
reading the land & sea
in this doubling up of things

the horizon recedes light retires
the pattern held for long
a form of shelter in the asymmetry

overhead sunless
when here in the rain
the sun gone

all twittering & busyness suspended
held as breath

the conditional swallowed down
but forever airborne
alive to movement

as if the blue scream that comes
from three-quarters behind the ear

in the daydreams of daytime
foreign & uncanny beam

where every song finds a corner a well

remembering all the dead people
left out with the moment gone
the unsung & the cloud

its signal & angels up here
in none none of the words above
singing into crying

at the doorway & gable-end
met in the triangulation

the personal & the social
the word after the moment of the late word
after

the dispersal into thin air

Leading Edge

to first signs in every aspect
read by streetlight

call out wandering & walk on
the chill first light of daybreak

like a gull call from the middle of the night

where moonlight shows itself
one last brightness
cut off point

is the knot in the not
& crowns for clowns
on the spot

& heart work
in what comes to a standstill
knocked back to origins

like the thinking of the sea
a place to go out & into
transition the present

the meaning in excess of the thing
between mirror & murmur
the state of the nomad

& the circus of order & chaos
interpret is to mean interrupt
the flower

elsewhere instantaneous
dwelling on the cusp
to reflect

roam
past the gate

in the form of an edge
& the wind is up
blue atmosphere ahead

like a load freighted with no truck
but to carry the image old & tired
draws a line

how walking affected thinking
an after life
& the walking continued

like the wing of an aircraft flexing

of precarious tilt & trick
to keep balance shaking chaos
& immediate

or crashing through upstairs rooms at midnight
from the window
snow across the tops last winter

a landscape network & notebook
tangled hearing it right
the edge of the idea

calling into the word
of last morning
the threshold & horizon

of correspondences to constellations
in rain & stone to solitary

dusted the mouth
of a grounded angel

the cold in the cold ground

as low cloud
the pull of the air
heat & insects rising

as tumblers gymnasts
outside the frame here outside

exit text the quiet places

waves
past the here of now

a place to go out into
the quivering edge

is to speak outside the noise
a full circle in magic & trapeze
in rotation or attention

of image & angel
& who comes through the door

to the letter & the day after tomorrow

of simple data & encounter
same shoes same trees same
earth visible from the moon

there will be no more dreams

& petals are parcels of light
& a world touched at every moment
a world touched into every moment

now a whisper
now song held
on the edge

on first view
the low light of liminal shiver

like the gods at last coming to earth
racing the sun as it drops away

Second Song Book: Series of Songs

Song: Call Centre

the song a form of call
to it where the poems sit

in the other room
out of reach of daybreak
& at the start of something

in the endless pattern of it
the meaning in the rainbow
the plan of it

the incomprehensible
lines of it
in the endless lines of it

in the rain

unknown remembered
remembered unknown

under lost murk
under muck of the republic

the lost track
static crackle to solar energy
all the rains & all the stones

Song: Lyrik

like a walk
use simple use
in a moment's crisis

language speaks simply where angels crowd in in the brokenness

then to follow the path
a patch to the field's edge
the house & its hours

a room for thinking
more than through
hum & vibration

the song back the mirror
put to air

the immediate distress
of address
the test

& years go by the emptied years

abandoned unrecorded
eclipsed cut out
a template or pattern

dreams / space / cellar / hut

interruption to song
like exile
the closeness of the breeze freezing

the argument spiral-bound
& as landscape
forms of lyric

lead to the view
fields gates tracks
or paths north

never the sun
a state of emergency

forms rooms
gathering clusters
resistance

a thin strip of air as the rain comes in
force-field or constellation suspended without

full energy
to quiver
into a mirror distortion

& reverberation
into shelter
folding over into shadow

the image before what is said
is song
haunted by hauntings

blocked or locked out

of echoes from other rooms
at the sign of lost gods
monuments

& other forms of error

Song: Edge

the face in the fact of it
& what rings
staged as an unfolding

in the sound of fairs & ice-cream vans
& all those forget-me-not blues
what forms 'your turn'

fragment
by fragment
precarious

& the knock on the downbeat
numb to number
the wind disturbs

tracking the moon continent to continent

clowns & angels in the conditional

lowered on to the living edge
all shipwreck returned
to think the day another abandoned day

the ship the bear & all the unborn
a blur of swifts
make good

Song: Response Unit

snowflakes are like fingerprints
an empty chain
to another high wire act

species & spaces
sings the wind
where sound rises to song

the night sky suspended in the wash of language
into the azure delicate as lyric
turning in the mouth

need at the fingertips
bit of a stretch

tyres over the surface
dead in the shriek of

high light on the farthest edge
these recorded in photographs
& those not

in the endless roads & tracks
in the kaleidoscope of ephemera
& music like rainwater

like reading the horoscope
winter flowering blossom
luminous & twilit

to the shape
the pleasures fewer
for clarity

startlingly
like a barn owl stunned & flopping on to tarmac

& the end disappears

Song: Tear

leaf turned

& on the up turn
imagined space
opening the encounter

in the off key of upheaval

& sing back
the poem's unreality

clouded
shadows leaves echoes flattened out
in black & white

is to contain or inhabit
brought to the edge

& discomfort
slower now but carried forward
into the shape into the house

when holding the moment like a frozen escalator
is to change the air
rinsed & clarified

the haunted Real outside
of black tree branches
black with rain at the window

a signature a dwelling place
& the dark floating by out there

the room sits empty
beside an empty sky

& what can never be known
of the screen

come out waving a white flag
& sway a last dance
weaving air

clouds & the gulls amongst them
deranged

of all the various forms
in all their variousness

like following a rail
or off the screen

the turn in the turn
is to constrain or inhibit

gone with the song
gone to the gable end

Charm

as paper is paper
in form
song o song

articulation
through unison
about touch

across air
air & space

ticking between sleep
for waking

Song Song Song

breaking hearts over an anvil

listening stations for the lost word
& language the spirit of the living
in the doing

threat & throat seemingly
the same root
singing the talk

into speech
in the pure version
a music like silence hidden in silence

the song breaking signal into broken

rains the everyday clear
& opaque
simultaneity

a form of words
& something to kick back with
along the lost track

the grey of heavy cloud
& no speaking part
a forgotten outpost

the miracle each living
specimen
lilt into an interval

the onlooker from afar
whose politics won't do
is to step aside

split into smithereens
the talk the song
into openings new

& now
to follow into the endless loop
of things

a rain cloud hanging in the air
& that's it

'the social contract on beauty'

a tidy enough looking coup
written into the endlessly blue

break out break away break

& the word after the late word
living amongst these lines
the lines of the living

embedded imperfections
& a change in direction
extends empathy with the object

the blue for weather the wet for snow

is to forge & forget
song snagged on song

side-step
with signs of movement

& signs of music
patrols & parrots

lost to the after-song
what then
home

replay echo & reply
to speech

the breakdown various & constant
the talk singing of talk

mists burning off
leaving the north station
about now

Song: Return

a lens lends an image
duet of dusts

equipment for Being-in-the-World
the tuning thing
turning against

landscape a cloud the dark
in the dirt of argument
known by walking cold air

marks a return to the home
not to the house
the strangeness sidelined

bends the focus
soon to be the sunning spot
inhabits earth & heart

stretched into a spaghetti of molecules

apart from breathing
another air space

a cold bed & a dim light
located & displaced
held at a bad signal

the equipment the implements
the mirror swallows the World
come to go

spade spanner spirit-level
forms of re-enactment

daylight night echoes tides

dead trees pulled to the sea on the outgoing
the World the mirror swallows

the silence of the house
without light no Universe
an image a lens lends

push on

Song: Likeness

in cycles encountered
& praise cadence
the steep

by association
past the point
or to detail

monitored heartland
borne up & out of
the metaphor

the step
at low tide
deaf

to the dead star
a sound

which will carry
a shadow window

aluminium crumpled
reflection to images
face close up

as a self-portrait
an attention to light
of no return

names number identities

these glittering arrangements
this fearful asymmetry
led to

& the sensation of flying
or falling or floating
airborne

is to write is to wander
frayed & frail

fragile misunderstandings
flake or crumble

overhead the overheard
breathy

unfolding

as the time does

to swim further out
beyond a dare

or the wish to
know
all worthwhile

ping & pearl counter
in the uncalled for
air

foil to dice
& prose
the steeple

Personal Song

done with thinking
& wet light after rain
asymmetric

tree / harbour / star
translated into sound

to follow the thread with the grain

to where the gods were lost
to where time empties now

displaces light
into the redness in redress

killing unicorns
always present
dwelling at the end moment

forge a leaving edge
forget the key

connected through the days
why & way

daybreak a kind of violence

in some blue light
images returning
a line of vision travels

divided & always receding
the air dripping
since sense

folding like with difference
pulse with silence
pulses against grain

what places what
displaces

the personal
the private dreamscape

space in the shape
of arches bridges
what tumbles out

air deranged trembles

violets / flagstone / chair

without circulation
in some blue light
the image returns

makes sense of the raining down
& dreaming of day

Shout: A Song

a shout is a song
& a leap is not

as a cutting wind
is to float off grid
is to ask of the stars

or the sound
& colours change
or the atom

the ghosts are sails & real

a ghost ship
witness in whiteness

flutter & not let up
reel off

is to read a newspaper
is to read a poem for news
like a hut

the turn & the twist
into the hurdy-gurdy
is to leap & not look

the light no longer clear & blue but grey
the troubled hours of waking & memory
sail said muffled with grey

the trail & the trial
in the tail of the tale

the wind turn
the travel north

the lines end the lines

Song: Mimesis

is the reach back
& round

like likening
like listening

as though by a siren pulled on
to disaster

landscape filled from the optic
mimetic

living inside winter
& the species
rain on air

like a typewriter mind
of personal expression

like a typewriter
motion to
trip & dance

with a sparrow
tighten the song
with a spanner the nut

to their shapes
speaking deeply
into darkest space

hollowed out

on paint & point of pain
this far

like that
ghost & air full of

every singular snowflake & birds all species

angled in from the wild
behind the wind & storm

by taking it to the end
radiance
map voice

the last space to speak from
like lightning

Postscript

opens a space that touches
the world at its edges
controlled space with the human voice

answers the world
in the light of that day

in the opened ground into the opened air
the cloud thought & presence of it
house of echoes bracket & pocket

the poem is a form of witchcraft
performed in the blue
of dawn & rain

& what kind of space does it unfold
what's left when everything else is taken

when beauty is not enough
politics too the environment
everywhere & always

agile
the poem a form
space pared back from perspective

the beat of the wave
& afterlife the receding glow

read back from history
spliced out of circumstance
out of the material language

to form an object
a thing out of context
& of politics

addressed to friends
Dorothy Nell Kat
call them

in the form of letters
through the after
words the cut-outs

& what counts

the future narrow narrows
as for the words 'use' or 'lose'

glitter & fade
these are the rules

drawn up like a chair
sat in & set four-square

just like a male's human head
on a mare's neck
what is true is the miracle

a woman a mermaid
or a moving shadow
of purple mauve

a mo*vie*

in medias res a Life process
a life opening
out

into the colour of sunshine
the variants of sunrise
& &

where the light falls the light fails
on the wavelength or song
forms a leaving edge leaving

theoreticians & academia to spit the feathers
painters poets to conjure chaos
ridiculous forms a menagerie

& sightlines out of nowhere
go forward where eyes (& ears) never go
particular as a fingerprint

blind as Oedipus was blinded
following the red road on the map

where there were no lies
not seeing the Truth before the eyes

the sound beneath the tongue
& pitch black
meaning forms towards the back of the head

like planting a fig-tree & what awaits names
the known
becoming new

of lambs & iambs
slipping out of earshot

followed out to where the air is clear

in off
& for the record
as it is *is* as it is

a pattern of chances made sense

the *ars poetica* is poetry's space
like painting forms of silence

caught in the moving light
moving colours

& somebody to say it
off stage & in character

who was there the companion
the angel
& the moon's endless changing shape

falling through the meaning
to pick up a thread
articulate the unsung the root

to map a route
a vision played with cards

the lyric sick as a doily
sick as the rocking motion of its simile
& maintain the act of song impossible

through the liminal spaces
where the metaphor is the ghost

an afterthought
the weave of the wave freestyling

the glance towards the golden section
like pointing
of brickwork & gesture

the poem is a form of colour of light

from red to blue
the shape & shadow together
mass & bulk

the beat of the spectrum
the stars gradually dispersed
dissolve into silence

the gauge & measure
sound echo of sound
& the sound that is echo

what goes & is gone
finally to silence & the empty

the after wave in the aftershock

& finally to echo
separated elements
push out unknown

what the human voice cannot take

how a song names
a few images on light on water
& what never stops

>*o little voice o little vase*
>*a broken cord in the broken*
>*chord*

one day folds over the next into asymmetry
hinge edge display
the news is breaking

flimsy as an index card
gone missing refracted

like water a glassful from the tap

out of life & in character
blank names to blank faces
suspended

like the silent fourth

pulled back into the immediate
by what magic is a person made
by which icy light

future from permanent blue
a cloud

but it doesn't stop loving
with listening to bodies
& listing things

what sharpens shapes
& straightens beds

feeling affect
after affection after affectation

item

'scribbled violet disc in venetian
with reds & emerald

September 1981'
to keep summer alive
for everyday use

by looking at the same thing again

then in this light
against this angle
to forge a leading edge

always falling forward
into beginning this moment
the last the first

& all the truth in the five acts
or three or twenty-four hours
or listening to the list

& the wound can never close
holding pattern
posthumous to the dead & sentimental

incoming add on
cold cold cold as the moon

observe articulate

Being comes from nowhere
but the language

through autumn & winter to spring
a lifetime epic
a Life

Love & language the same thing
new poems like tears

the what *is* is simple & delight
pure just say it into the microphone
as though life depended on it

the space is one
of intimacy
balanced in asymmetry

lost to the dazzle
& vertical light horizontal light

where the language is before
it comes over into articulation
& intimacy

what thought might leave anonymous
the colour grey

& this the best of illusions
to defamiliarise the gaze
not a bit like a horse's head

like reflections on mud waterlogged
where the implements become impediments
quits & quilts

speaking difficulty
coming to love the words late

speaks into the space
speaks into the entry
speaks into

entanglements blue as shadow
impossible what the poem stands for
a return to reading the world

& the what will never be known

as I read the words
but cannot see the rain
remembering to feel happy

Drafts & Fragments

Song: Cuttings

just over into leaf
luminous as gold

on the other side
birds are louder

what just falls
beyond the frame

narrows
in the rain

flag of surrender
a boat a marble boat

peacocks & lions
of the pleasure boats & tourists

chasing daylight
at border checks
& silent cloud

hear in the rain
bleached off-white

reel to Real
unbroken surface

off the World
walking off
a place of execution

of mottled bark
& red parasol

frame by frame

by frame
rain beaten dust
to close not end

Passages Passengers

trees sing their own songs

an area flares up an aura
at the boundaries at the edge

into an anatomy a chord
strictures of song

what goes on as background noise
patterning decoration adornment
where the stars will come

to structure no harm
to name

in a name
light reflected out
of reflection there lies chance

the work of light
from this mid-summer point

the days draw in
on yellow-green leaves cabbage white
a dull light at risk of change

the light of a pool
in the light of a wristwatch
in the light of a ceiling

vowels like flowers to speech
like vouchers to the modern epoch

tines with an idea
for one or two reasons & a tune

given up for a song
passengers follow their own passages

the quiet the city the sky
don't blink
reading the dial

reading the soil
like mystery like enchantment

through the teeth
through the lips

through the out breath

& then what
noted with blue pencil

scorched grasses & lavender hostages to bee-works
resonate erasure with reason where the fall is

exchange
wrapped around the energy buzz

particles particulates part the particular
inching forward through the night
the sound of a door closing

a door shut a star
a small point of light
star shadow of a sun

& pressing the buttons of the lift
where does the heart appear
when does the heart appear

in a name from a home to the anatomy
of song in beeswax

substitute coriander for corridor
passengers for hostages
stanzas for machine guns

a dead planet the stars above
& is this all happening now

an iceberg's thunder & the World
vanishing vanishing

Being & they are not
dizzy or off balance
connected by a wristwatch

itch with no idea
where the storm will

& this is all happening now
Being in love with the World
the habitable planet not far above

the chestnut trees burnt out already
leaves crackle secrets
like blown filaments

the origins of the name in a sign
habitable

as I rush towards my end
crash out of Being
where the storm will

these are the best of things
vanishing point vanishing

the origins of a sign in a name
the anatomy of song
the architecture of song

the stars stare back blankly
from the structure
the blue window

on a crescent on a single voice
on a song

Song: Triangle

the deranged air
the changed air

to spell out a triangle like a ringtone

Reverie

the way & the why a Fool feels
awake without end alive to

out of space
have say ruin

on radio for the wavelengths

or what floats by with the air
& dips
leaf in the off key

the river will be wiped
returned to elements

as natural light fails led away to rooms

hitched to the uncertain luminous
in the resemblance of balance
marks & works

the reverie with all slap dash velocity
terms & conditions attached

reached for
the outstretch of sycamore
or the politics of maple

& other forms of hinged

Reality
switched in the "on" position
to contain attention

dawn / shadow / caller / house

ruined elements
unconvinced as the World
becomes an hostile environment

burst the image
bust the cloud

switched in the rain
by what magic
quivers with light

the function & where to start

deep to the interior

as good as song
as good as that

Vital Signs

sinking chill of air
like reading music

hinge echo display
to no true end point
& exile

the whole chorus & circus while
lost in the dazzle
& shimmer

the moment the envelope the step forward
hardly a day

or the hut where all the energy is bound

to keep looking & dwelling
in a kind of reclaiming
in the agile moment

as though too soon to make sense

when to dwell is to contain
in some blue light

the electricity a form of magic
field fluid fold
& gone

when like a farmhouse on a hill
the images return
taken to heart

from the outskirts
of dissent
overscored

door / sunrise / construction / heaven

a top road to the lyric house
the light arrives
after fifty years out

Envelope

echoes are angels
by this shore the margin
like a poem forgotten

that space
abandonment
admits light

as though about to listen
& making sense of Self
as the words drift out

Time dead knowledge gone
the gods lost
opening the light

blue over white
another form of words
just out of reach lost to touch

the lyre in lyric & lure to oversight

the not-quite-random
thin film of rain
singing & signing out

is to go away to feel close

Private Poem

scent is presence
welcomed to night

& facing the sun's hum
no escaping eternity

folded into the eternal
eyes wet

Song

specimen is a detour
time unattached
a nearness

a beautiful smell
clouded
a beautiful scent

ghostly that ghost
a term

reality of day
a dreamscape

All Schubert

takes breath
lower registers lower
under the order of light

becomes a lie
until the batteries fail
& the nick of time

a notch caught in the bark
with the cutting
chalk the other side

tracing company
until silence
& with the voice

forms a gate

After After-Effects

the water & the very air owned
is to lead the witness

& the days flicker away so fast
they explode with hail pellets
later splash as rain droplets

down gutters down waste pipes
flood drains flush seaward
& away so out to sea

is to be lost within oversight not Love & walk away unharmed

lucked out & lost as much
as telling

sorrows across the waters
time enough where past collapses into futures
where reflection is captured in one drop of rain

the elements of the lament patterned naming in the air
in the show of hands
the authentic

lumpen & shapeless
where no lies follow & awake from winter easy as that
with the meanings scored out

with what lies in the lyric
cloud suspended

locked out of social contact
Time attached to the air
or draw a blank

Personal Poem

in all the receptions corridors & waiting rooms leading in
the chambers of the heart like bedrooms in a hotel
with a day & everything moving slowly

moving more slowly after song after song
the vital signs for a season
variable length

snags & songs
from the heart

images without title without echo
chambers but tissue between shadows
through vestibules

fusing the view together shadow to object

shadow without object

as removed from personal experience to a petri dish
& without subtitles
return alone

as arguments follow tracks
throw dice instead

no "I" lives here measuring call
when without scent twice removed
the movement of capital to the edges

when this should be an 'Ode to Joy' sung out

while this is spoken in the speaking
a serious game about measure & emotion
sing song sing

Sonnet

in the small room where it begins
in the press of language
forward

over a new threshold
through the opaque air
on & through the synthetic city air

through the ear buds to the sinister "tin tin" of the 1890s Erard
to Satie's 'Gnossiennes'
in the anteroom awaiting the waiting

& the breathing of a new breath
to form an interior life
by the energy & the connection

after the Métro
Ligne 4 to arise at Vavin
under Balzac's cloak

in the direction of Mairie Montrouge
after the vestibule
disembarkation

the spaces like pauses
like the spaces between spaces spaces
the antechamber after that

after the carriage rolls rolled like a ship on the slow waltz
& to arise to open air
to breathe out the opaque air

& to the pasts with their consequences
& the slow wave

as the white bark of the silver birch
true as that interlocutor

fainter & fainter
all the receptions corridors & waiting
rooms leading in

the chambers of the heart
& the bedrooms the hotel rooms

along the Boulevard du Montparnasse
the Novanox through habit Le Royal by booking error

de la Paix to lay with Sartre de Beauvoir Breton
Hôtel Atelier Saint-Germain by chance
Mercure Paris Montparnasse with pleasure

a tear in the cloud inconsolable
from this small room it sets out

laid out airwaves as song
of exhaled obvious air

with a day
& everything moving slowly
moving more slowly song after

song after song the vital signs for a season of variable length
in the small room where it happens

as the rain
spatters like the sound of grains
sand across flat rooftops snags & songs

if there were snow it would be luminous
if there were soft snow
but there is no snow there is rain

& where they're leading from the heart

careering round this city in a circle
finishing up where it finishes up
without location

Chez Ferdinand gone
images without title without echo
a bed a beat of the heart

curtains drawn translate into blocked sleep
hubbub like rhubarb at the window
with the poem a form of hideout

chambers in series in miseries in misery in misericords
in mimicry

the constantly happening
forward the insistence without delay
flicking the tops of discourse

of forests of tall buildings & not so tall
all but tissue between shadows
through the vestibules of hotels & lodgings

the song as essential
waiting intervals awaiting
hand on heart

FaceTime on the Left Bank

to ring down & through time
horizon in line the earth in darkness
through the Jardin du Luxembourg

some form of original signal
some form

the living between news bulletins
the view fusing together
shadow to object

& all the equipment in place
follow where the word goes
its permanent signal

Rilke its satellite
lighthouse to the heart
marker & distress

signal
at the coast & edge
outside identifiable place

to be one day picked out of the Channel

immanent contingent
the cables & joints of this voice
speaking out loud to lyric

expressing self-regard lyric to the core

outside identities
the constant loss of touch
shadow without object

as far as the atrium
removed from personal experience to a petri dish
& without subtitles

return alone
as arguments follow tracks inside

throw dice instead & then the alarms

no "I" lives here measuring call

when without scent twice removed
the movement of capital to the edges

when this should be an 'Ode to Joy' sung out
not a monument

while this is spoken in the speaking
has taken place enacted
to forge & forage

a serious game about measure & emotion
has taken place
sing song sing

Song: Pattern/No Reply/Detour/
Untrodden Path/Further Afield

the cordoned warehouses
kilometres of barb-wired track

From the Heart

& so home across the fields

a suspension of disbelief
without notes too far felt

on the corner decision
opens up the air

maybe eyes blown visions coming down
intimate as snow neutral light
a sky turning turquoise then grey

a city of hardware hard facts underscored

by what magic is a person made
when from the heart

hinge threshold shadow
its infinite perspective

to the edge the cornea
if you still maintain the attention of the sitter
the heart a shift in gear

maybe a whole other level
of understanding

maybe one line
of cloud formation

one cold front
meets warmer air

maybe other lives
over the land & real

maybe talk forms a state
& dips away
late or later

disappears into

Zone

at the end you're bored with this ageing world

herdswoman O Eiffel Tower the flock of bridges bleat this morning

you are at the end of your tether with these Greek & Roman ways

at this point even the horseless carriage appears Old World
only religion stands out original religion
stands straight up as the aircraft hangers at Port Aviation

On the Edges of Air

pronouns shifted around the scene or into the wings
the voice laying down in the law
speaking persistence

take a breather
out for some air
like it's a first date

the self-regarding porous & a halo into life

organic as a letter these are edge technologies

the term 'quest' in the question question
the present crisis ever present
as language marks the break the crisis

queasy at the line the hill path takes watching along the edge

lark from the ground
to sky unzips the landscape no longer
a still chill to the air

ghost birch suspended & the feint boom of traffic
steals the half-remembered voice
where did solitude tip to loneliness

whistled & run in its opposite direction

then there's the whole thing
pulled into life again & reaching out for the edge

never say a simile again never
the nowhere now here
the agility of

the silence of still air
hear some fragment
of song

read the sky slowly
airborne song

me yes me escapes the bombardment of data

pulls clear & threadbare
in a stolen voice

Alive

goes with the saying
the "if" in proliferation in life in lift

& the sky moves silent & unmeasured
"live" in the present tense

the contaminated air of song

the body all that is left
or maybe shadow

Lyric Bird

take the lyric bird
gathered voice

the private & universal
lyric close to "like"
& supply lines

Pocket: Song

a shelter & a secret
a shifter

is to stand outside time
a ticket stub a laundry receipt
a micro-story

painted from memory
to seal & conceal
working on paper walking on

as a poem is a pocket & swifts' nest

a home a dwelling an echo chamber
constructed from mud

& the cord is flying
as the scaffold breaks the sightline
under the house eave

air delicate habitat fragile

language a category of poetry fallen
from grace into a slouch
hands in pockets

sudden arrivals May made for departures September
& two broods between
twin pockets

& to overwrite its secrets
eyes open mouth open
pillow of cloud

a cadence
as background information
all neat full & enclosed

carries through sound carries through

the weather & how to survive it
carries a packet lost in a pocket
of time

the swifts the screamers
precipitous migrant answerless

branded 'a pastoral' to leaf

cradle
sounding as though hidden secret

warm to warm the hands chilled

to fall short
aloud to fail homing
is to carry with care

how would a poem help
how much a pocket contain

a stanza is a room
tuned to a watering-can

Acknowledgments

Several of these poems were written during research leave in Spring 2018 from the University of Kent, in London, Hope Cove, Ramsgate & Beijing. Other poems were written on a writing retreat at Ferrybridge in Wales in July 2019. I want to thank the University of Kent for financial support during the research leave & retreat in 2018 and 2019. 'Post-Political Love Poem,' 'Elegy: On the End of Ending,' 'Fairground' & 'Emergency Attention' first appeared in *Molly Bloom* 22. A big thank you to Aidan Semmens for his enthusiasm for and attention to these poems.

These poems were written between December 2017 and August 2019. This book is for Felicity Allen.

About the Author

Simon Smith has published nine collections of poetry. His third, *Mercury* (Salt Publications), was long-listed for the Costa Prize in 2007. A selected poems, *More Flowers Than You Could Possibly Carry*, appeared from Shearsman Books in 2016, and his latest books are some *Municipal Love Poems* (Muscaliet Press) and *Day In Day Out* (Parlor Press), and his translations of Catullus were published by Carcanet as *The Books of Catullus*. These three books were published in 2018. Smith is Reader in Creative Writing at the University of Kent, was a Hawthornden Writing Fellow in 2009, and a judge of the National Poetry Prize in 2004. From 1991-2007 he worked at The Poetry Library in London, becoming Librarian from 2003-2007. Recently poems have appeared in *Shearsman*, *Fortnightly Review* and *Molly Bloom*, from an unpublished book, *Midnight Arks*. He is now an editor for Free Verse online magazine. He is presently also translating a selection of poems by Du Fu.

Photograph of the author by Felicity Allen. Used by permission.

Free Verse Editions

Edited by Jon Thompson

13 ways of happily by Emily Carr
& in Open, Marvel by Felicia Zamora
Alias by Eric Pankey
Ariadne, A Series by Martha Ronk
At Your Feet (A Teus Pés) by Ana Cristina César, edited by Katrina Dodson, trans. by Brenda Hillman and Helen Hillman
Bari's Love Song by Kang Eun-Gyo, translated by Chung Eun-Gwi
Between the Twilight and the Sky by Jennie Neighbors
Blood Orbits by Ger Killeen
The Bodies by Christopher Sindt
The Book of Isaac by Aidan Semmens
The Calling by Bruce Bond
Canticle of the Night Path by Jennifer Atkinson
Child in the Road by Cindy Savett
Civil Twilight by Giles Goodland
Condominium of the Flesh by Valerio Magrelli, trans. by Clarissa Botsford
Contrapuntal by Christopher Kondrich
Country Album by James Capozzi
Cry Baby Mystic by Daniel Tiffany
The Curiosities by Brittany Perham
Current by Lisa Fishman
Day In, Day Out by Simon Smith
Dear Reader by Bruce Bond
Dismantling the Angel by Eric Pankey
Divination Machine by F. Daniel Rzicznek
Elsewhere, That Small by Monica Berlin
Empire by Tracy Zeman
Erros by Morgan Lucas Schuldt
Fifteen Seconds without Sorrow by Shim Bo-Seon, trans. by Chung Eun-Gwi and Brother Anthony of Taizé
The Forever Notes by Ethel Rackin
The Flying House by Dawn-Michelle Baude
Ghost Letters by Baba Badji
Go On by Ethel Rackin
Here City by Rick Snyder
Instances: Selected Poems by Jeongrye Choi, trans. by Brenda Hillman, Wayne de Fremery, & Jeongrye Choi
Last Morning by Simon Smith

The Magnetic Brackets by Jesús Losada, trans. by M. Smith & L. Ingelmo
Man Praying by Donald Platt
A Map of Faring by Peter Riley
The Miraculous Courageous by Josh Booton
Mirrorforms by Peter Kline
No Shape Bends the River So Long by Monica Berlin & Beth Marzoni
North | Rock | Edge by Susan Tichy
Not into the Blossoms and Not into the Air by Elizabeth Jacobson
Overyellow, by Nicolas Pesquès, translated by Cole Swensen
Parallel Resting Places by Laura Wetherington
Physis by Nicolas Pesquès, translated by Cole Swensen
Pilgrimage Suites by Derek Gromadzki
Pilgrimly by Siobhán Scarry
Poems from above the Hill & Selected Work by Ashur Etwebi, trans. by Brenda Hillman & Diallah Haidar
The Prison Poems by Miguel Hernández, trans. by Michael Smith
Puppet Wardrobe by Daniel Tiffany
Quarry by Carolyn Guinzio
remanence by Boyer Rickel
Republic of Song by Kelvin Corcoran
Rumor by Elizabeth Robinson
Settlers by F. Daniel Rzicznek
Signs Following by Ger Killeen
Small Sillion by Joshua McKinney
Split the Crow by Sarah Sousa
Spine by Carolyn Guinzio
Spool by Matthew Cooperman
Strange Antlers by Richard Jarrette
Summoned by Guillevic, trans. by Monique Chefdor & Stella Harvey
Sunshine Wound by L. S. Klatt
System and Population by Christopher Sindt
These Beautiful Limits by Thomas Lisk
They Who Saw the Deep by Geraldine Monk
The Thinking Eye by Jennifer Atkinson
This History That Just Happened by Hannah Craig
An Unchanging Blue: Selected Poems 1962–1975 by Rolf Dieter Brinkmann, trans. by Mark Terrill
Under the Quick by Molly Bendall
Verge by Morgan Lucas Schuldt
The Visible Woman by Allison Funk
The Wash by Adam Clay

We'll See by Georges Godeau, trans. by Kathleen McGookey
What Stillness Illuminated by Yermiyahu Ahron Taub
Winter Journey [Viaggio d'inverno] by Attilio Bertolucci, trans. by Nicholas Benson
Wonder Rooms by Allison Funk

CPSIA information can be obtained
at www.ICGtesting.com
Printed in the USA
BVHW071606161121
621779BV00004B/174